Minutes

Nita Mehta

B.Sc. (Home Science), M.Sc. (Food and Nutrition)
Gold Medalist

SNAB

COOK in minutes

© Copyright 2007-2008 SNAB Publishers Pvt Ltd

Reprint 2008
ISBN 978-81-7869-116-9

Food Styling and Photography: SNAB

Layout and laser typesetting :

National Information Technology Academy
N.I.T.A. 3A/3, Asaf Ali Road, New Delhi-110002
☎ 23252948

Published by :

SNAB

Publishers Pvt. Ltd.
3A/3 Asaf Ali Road,
New Delhi - 110002
Tel: 23252948, 23250091
Telefax:91-11-23250091

Editorial and Marketing office:
E-159, Greater Kailash-II, N.Delhi-48
Fax: 91-11-29225218, 29229558
Tel: 91-11-29214011, 29218727, 29218574
E-Mail: nitamehta@email.com
nitamehta@nitamehta.com
Website: http://www.nitamehta.com
Website: http://www.snabindia.com

Contributing Writers :
Anurag Mehta
Subhash Mehta

Editorial & Proofreading :
Rakesh
Ramesh

Distributed by :

THE VARIETY BOOK DEPOT
A.V.G. Bhavan, M 3 Con Circus,
New Delhi - 110 001
Tel : 23417175, 23412567; Fax : 23415335
Email: varietybookdepot@rediffmail.com

Printed by :

PARAS OFFSET PVT. LTD.
C-176, Naraina, Phase-I, New Delhi

Rs. 89/-

INTRODUCTION

Cooking in minutes is easy if you are well organised in the kitchen, with a ready stock of those essential ingredients that save time – for example, readymade tomato puree, packaged cream, readymade coconut milk, evaporated milk, canned or frozen corn and peas. Have family favourites like paneer, mushroom, pastas and boiled potatoes readily available.

In today's world where a woman has to play so many roles – wife, mother, hostess and career woman – she needs to be efficient and quick, while keeping an eye on all the different needs of her family. This book has recipes which will allow you to rush into your kitchen, pick up available ingredients of your choice and rustle up a tasty, nutritive, wholesome, jhatpat, 'meal in minutes'!

Nita Mehta

C O N T

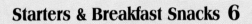

Starters
& Breakfast
Snacks

Crispy Seviyaan

Curry leaves and spices enliven these quick-cooking fine vermicelli (seviyaan) – a hearty and delicious breakfast.

Serves 4

2 cups (200 gm) Bambino vermicelli (*seviyaan*), 2 tsp salt, 1 tsp oil, 3 tbsp oil

1 tsp cumin seeds (*jeera*), 1 tsp mustard seeds (*sarson*), a few curry leaves

¼ tsp turmeric (*haldi*), juice of 1 large lemon

1¼ tsp salt, or to taste, ¼ cup chopped coriander

1 tbsp each of split gram dal (*channa dal*) and split black beans (*dhuli urad dal*) - soaked

for 15 minutes in warm water, 2-3 dry red chillies - broken into pieces, 1 onion - chopped

CRISPY CURRY PATTAS (CURRY LEAVES)

1 tbsp oil, ¼ cup curry leaves (5-6 sprigs) - washed and pat dried on a clean kitchen towel

---

1. Boil 8 cups of water with 2 tsp salt and 1 tsp oil. Add seviyaan and cook just for 2-3 minutes till tender. Refresh in cold water several times (like the way you do for noodles). Strain and keep aside.

2. Heat oil in a kadhai. Reduce heat. Add the jeera and sarson and stir to mix. Wait till jeera turns light golden.

3. Add curry leaves and red chillies.

4. Add chopped onion and cook on low heat till it turns light brown.

5. Drain the water from the dals and add to the onions. Stir for 2 minutes or till dals turn soft.

6. Add haldi and mix well.

7. Add boiled seviyaan. Add lemon juice, salt and coriander leaves. Mix well and transfer to a serving dish. Keep aside.

8. Heat 1 tbsp oil in a small kadhai. Add ¼ cup curry leaves (leaves from 5-6 sprigs). Remove from fire. Stir. Wait for a minute till leaves turn crisp. Spoon the crisp leaves on the ready seviyaan in the dish.

Note: If using rice seviyaan, do not boil them. Simply soak them in hot water for 2-3 minutes till soft. Then refresh in cold water.

Apple Cheese Toasts

Serves 4-6

2 large apples, 1 tbsp butter

juice of 1 lemon (2 tbsp), 1 tbsp honey, ½ tsp pepper - freshly crushed

3-4 cheese cubes - grated (10-12 tbsp)

8 slices brown or white bread - toasted and buttered lightly, mint leaves - to garnish

1. Cut apples into thin slices along with the peel. Melt butter in a non stick pan and add the apple slices, lemon juice, and honey. Cook on low flame for about 1-2 minutes, till apples get coated with butter. Sprinkle pepper & mix. Keep aside.

2. Arrange apple slices on the buttered toast, to cover the toast almost completely.

3. Grate about ½ cube of cheese (2 tbsp) on the apples. Sprinkle a pinch of freshly crushed peppercorns.

4. Heat oven to 210°C and put the toasts on the wire rack of the oven to grill the toasts for about 5 minutes. Garnish with mint leaves. Serve.

Pizza Margherita Squares

A classic pizza, named after the Italian Queen - "Margherita. You can add any combination of cut vegetables on it like capsicum, tomatoes, onion, corn etc. Cut it into squares and serve as a starter.

Makes 2 pizzas

2 ready made pizza bases

TOMATO SAUCE

250 gm tomatoes - blanched (put in hot water and peeled) and chopped finely

½ cup ready-made tomato puree, 4-5 flakes garlic - crushed, 1 tbsp oil

1 bay leaf, ½ tsp vinegar, salt & freshly ground pepper to taste, 1 tsp dried oregano

TOPPING

10-12 fresh basil leaves - roughly chopped

150 gm mozzarella or pizza cheese - cut into thin slices or grated (1½ cups), 2 tbsp olive oil

1. For tomato sauce, heat 1 tbsp oil in a pan. Add garlic. Stir and add all other ingredients. Boil. Simmer on low heat for 10 minutes, stirring occasionally until it is reduced in quantity and thick enough to spread without being runny.

2. Spoon the prepared tomato sauce over each pizza base, leaving ½" all around the edges.

3. Brush the edges with olive oil. Sprinkle with half the basil leaves. Arrange cheese slices or grated cheese on top of the pizza. Drop few drops of sauce over the pizza.

4. Drizzle 1 tbsp olive oil on the cheese and bake in a pre-heated oven on the wire rack (not tray) at 180°C (350°F) for 15 minutes or until the base is evenly browned and the cheese gets melted.

5. Repeat with the remaining ingredients to make another pizza. Cut into squares to serve.

Hariyaali Idlis

Make green idlis by adding pureed spinach to the batter. Wrap them in curd, and temper the dish with spices, tomatoes and curry leaves.

Serves 8

1 packet (200 gm) ready-made idli mix

1½ cups chopped spinach, ½ tsp salt

2-3 green chillies - deseeded & chopped

a few cashewnuts or blanched almonds - split into two halves, optional

TOPPING

2 cups fresh curd - beat well till smooth, ½ tsp salt

TEMPERING (*TADKA*)

2 tbsp oil, 1 tsp small brown mustard seeds (*rai*)

½ tsp cumin seeds (*jeera*)

2 green chillies - chopped

1 small tomato - chopped finely

20-30 curry leaves

1. Mix the idli mix according to the instructions on the packet.

2. Grind the chopped spinach and green chillies in a mixer and grind to a smooth puree or a paste with 1-2 tbsp water.

3. Add the spinach paste to the idli mixture. Add ½ tsp salt to it.

4. Grease a mini idli mould. Put a little batter in each cup and top with a split cashewnut or almond on each idli. Steam for 14-15 minutes on medium flame till a knife inserted in the idli comes out clean. If a mini mould is not available, make small flat idlis by putting a little less batter in the normal idli mould.

5. Place the steamed idlis in a large bowl.

6. Beat the curd with salt till smooth. Pour the curd over the idlis in the bowl. Mix gently. Keep aside for 10-15 minutes.

7. Transfer the idlis to a flat serving platter or a shallow dish.

8. Heat 2 tbsp oil. Add rai and jeera. When they stop spluttering, add green chillies, tomato and curry leaves. Stir to mix all ingredients and immediately pour over the idlis covered with curd. Serve.

Onion Rings

This atta-cornflour batter has just the right consistency and flavour – dip onion or capsicum rings, baby corns and mushrooms and deep-fry till crisp and golden.

Serves 4-6

2-3 large onions, a pinch of red chilli flakes

¼ cup whole wheat flour (*atta*), ¼ cup cornflour

¼ tsp garlic paste

1 tsp lemon juice, ½ tsp each salt, pepper and oregano

1. Cut onion into thick slices. Separate slices to get rings. Dip them in cold water and keep aside for ½ hour.

2. Make a thick coating batter with all other ingredients. Keep aside for 10 minutes.

3. Drain the onions. Wipe dry the onions on a kitchen towel. Heat oil. Dip onion rings in batter and deep fry 5-6 pieces at a time till golden and crisp. Remove from oil and drain on paper napkins. Serve with ketchup.

Quick Paneer Bites

Serves 3-4

200 gm paneer cut into ¼" thick, triangular pieces, sprinkle chat masala on paneer

BATTER

4 tbsp flour (*maida*), 2-3 flakes garlic - crushed, 1/3 cup water (approx.)

½ tsp chilli powder, ½ tsp chaat masala, ½ tsp salt to taste, a pinch carom seeds (*ajwain*)

COATING

1/3 cup bread crumbs, 4 tbsp sesame seeds (*til*), 1 tbsp semolina (*suji*)

pinch of dry orange red colour, oil for frying

1. Mix all the ingredients of the batter in a shallow flat bowl.

2. Mix all the coating ingredients in large flat plate, to spread out the mixture.

3. Dip the paneer pieces in the batter. Remove from batter and toss in the coating mixture to coat all sides. Fry the paneer pieces, one at a time, till crisp. Drain on paper napkins to absorb excess oil. Serve hot.

Indian
Curries

Dum Aloo Chutney Wale

An amazing gravy with tangy chutney mixed in a yogurt-cashew base – these potatoes win the first prize!

Serves 2- 3

2 potatoes - each cut into 4 cubes or 8 baby potatoes - keep whole

HARI CHUTNEY (GRIND TOGETHER)

1 cup chopped fresh coriander

½ small raw mango or ½ tsp dry mango powder (*amchoor*)

½ cup mint (*poodina*), ½ tsp salt, ½ tsp sugar

GRAVY

4 tbsp oil

1 tsp cumin (*jeera*) seeds, 2 onions - ground to a paste

4 tsp ginger- garlic paste, 1 tsp red chilli powder

1 cup yoghurt and 2 tbsp cashewnuts (*kaju*) - ground to a paste till smooth

1 cup water, 1 tsp salt, or to taste

1 tomato - chopped finely, ½ tsp garam masala

1. Peel and wash potatoes. Cut into cubes. Heat oil in a kadhai and deep fry over low heat until cooked and light brown.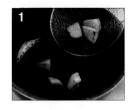

2. For gravy, grind cashews and yoghurt to a smooth paste.

3. Heat oil in a kadhai. Add jeera, wait for a minute till golden.

4. Add onion paste, stir over low heat until transparent. Do not brown the onions.

5. Add the ginger garlic paste and stir until the masala leaves oil.

6. Add yoghurt and cashews paste. Stir for 1- 2 minutes.

7. Add hari chutney and red chilli powder. Stir till oil separates and the mixture turns dry.

8. Add 1 cup water, stirring continuously on low heat till it comes to a boil.

9. Now add the fried potatoes and salt. Simmer uncovered for 5 minutes until the oil leaves the masala and the gravy turns thick.

10. Add chopped tomato and garam masala, stir and bring to a boil. Serve.

Note: Do not cover the kadhai while cooking, as yogurt or milk based gravies can curdle if covered while cooking.

Palak Chaman

Pureed spinach becomes transformed with a range of balancing spices. It is gently thickened with gram flour. (besan).

Serves 4

500 gm spinach (*palak*) - chopped (5 cups)

4 tbsp dry fenugreek leaves (*kasoori methi*), 1 cup chopped coriander, 1 green chilli

1 tsp sugar, 2 tbsp gram flour (*besan*), 250 gms paneer- cut into 1" pieces

½ stick cinnamon (*dalchini*), 2 green cardamoms (*chhoti elaichi*), 3-4 cloves (*laung*)

5 tbsp oil, 2 onions - ground to a paste, ½ cup cream or milk, approx., 1 tsp salt, or to taste

BAGHAR

1 tbsp desi ghee, 1 tbsp chopped ginger, ½ tsp red chilli powder

1. Boil spinach, kasoori methi, fresh coriander and green chilli in 1 cup water with sugar. Cook on low flame for 4-5 minutes till spinach turns soft. Remove from fire. Strain the spinach and keep liquid aside. Cool the spinach and blend to a puree.

2. Mix besan with the spinach liquid and keep aside.

3. Crush dalchini, laung and seeds of chhoti elaichi to a rough powder. Keep aside.

4. Heat 5 tbsp oil. Add onions and cook on low heat till oil separates and they turn light brown.

5. Add the freshly ground masala. Cook for a few seconds.

6. Add besan dissolved in liquid. Cook for 2 minutes.

7. Add the palak puree. Bhuno for 5-7 minutes till dry and oil separates.

8. Add enough cream or milk, to get the right consistency and colour. Cook on low heat for 2 minutes.

9. Add paneer pieces.

10. Add salt to taste. Simmer for a few minutes. Transfer to a serving dish.

11. To serve, heat 1 tbsp desi ghee for the baghar. Add ginger. Remove from fire. When ginger turns golden, add red chilli powder to the hot oil. Remove from fire and mix lightly with the spinach. Serve hot.

Shahi Baby Corns

This shahi red masala is rich with cashews and almonds, fragrant with cardamom and black cumin – to give baby corns the royal treatment! If baby corns are not available, corn on the cob may be used instead.

Serves 8

200 gm baby corns

MASALA

2 small onions, 4 tomatoes, ½" piece ginger, 1 green chilli, 4 tbsp oil

½ tsp black cumin (*shah jeera*), 1 tsp coriander (*dhania*) powder, ½ tsp amchoor

1½ tsp salt, ½ tsp red chilli powder, 1 tsp garam masala

2 tbsp cashews - soaked for 10 minutes and ground to a paste with ¼ cup water

1 tsp tandoori masala, optional, 2-3 green cardamom (*chhoti elaichi*) - seeds crushed

50-100 gm paneer - grated (½ -1 cup), 3 tbsp chopped coriander

BAGHAR OR TEMPERING

1 tbsp oil, ½ tsp black cumin (*shah jeera*), 1 tsp finely chopped ginger

5-6 almonds (*badaam*) - cut into thin long pieces, ¼ tsp red chilli powder

1. Keep baby corns whole. If thick, slit each piece into half lengthwise.

2. Blend onions, tomatoes, green chilli and ginger to a paste in a grinder.

3. Heat oil. Add shah jeera. After a minute, add onion-tomato paste and cook till dry and oil separates. Reduce flame. Add red chilli powder, dhania, amchoor, salt and garam masala. Cook for 1 minute.

4. Add cashew paste. Stir to mix well. Keeping the flame low, add baby corns, stirring continuously. Stir for 2-3 minutes.

5. Add enough (2 cups approx.) water to get a gravy. Boil. Simmer covered for 5-7 minutes till slightly thick and oil separates. Add tandoori masala, chhoti elaichi, paneer and coriander. Mix well.

6. Transfer to a serving dish. Heat oil. Add jeera and ginger. After a few seconds, add almonds and stir. Add red chilli powder, remove from fire and pour the oil on the gravy. Serve.

Malai Mushroom Matar

This milk-based, fragrant gravy will not overpower the delicacy of mushrooms and peas – a gourmet-class dish made in minutes.

Serves 4-5

200 gm mushrooms - preferably small in size

1 cup shelled, boiled or frozen peas, 4 tbsp kasoori methi (dry fenugreek leaves)

1 tsp ginger-garlic paste, a pinch of pepper, 1 tbsp butter, 3 tbsp oil

2 onions - ground to a paste

¼ cup malai (milk topping) - mix with ¼ cup milk and blend in a mixer for a few seconds till smooth or

½ cup thin fresh cream, 1 tsp salt to taste, ½ tsp red chilli powder, ½ tsp garam masala

a pinch of amchoor, ½ cup milk (approx.)

GRIND TOGETHER

½ stick cinnamon (*dalchini*), seeds of 2-3 green cardamom (*chhoti elaichi*)

3-4 laung (cloves), 4-5 peppercorns (*saboot kali mirch*)

2 tbsp roasted gram (*bhuna channa*) or cashewnuts

1. Trim the stem of each mushroom. Leave them whole if small or cut them into 2 pieces, if big. Heat 1 tbsp butter in a kadhai and add the mushrooms. Stir fry on high flame till dry and golden. Add 1 tsp ginger-garlic paste, ½ tsp salt and a pinch of black pepper. Stir for 1 more minute and remove from fire. Keep cooked mushrooms aside.

2. Grind together dalchini, seeds of chhoti elaichi, laung, kali mirch and channa/ cashew to a powder in a small mixer grinder.

3. Heat 3 tbsp oil. Add onion paste & cook on low heat till oil separates. Do not let the onions turn brown.

4. Add the freshly ground masala powder. Cook for a few seconds.

5. Add kasoori methi and malai, cook on low heat for 2-3 minutes till malai dries.

6. Add salt, red chilli powder, garam masala and amchoor. Stir for 1 minute.

7. Add the boiled peas and mushrooms.

8. Add ½ cup milk to get a thick gravy. Add ½ cup water if the gravy appears too thick. Boil for 2-3 minutes. Serve.

Quick Rajmah Curry

Red kidney beans in a tomato-based gravy are pressure cooked twice for quick and creamy results.

Serves 4-6

1½ cups red kidney beans (*lal rajmah*) - soaked overnight

1 tbsp split gram (*channe ki dal*) - soaked overnight

2 tsp salt or to taste, 1 onion - chopped finely

6-8 flakes garlic - crushed

1" piece ginger - chopped finely

4 tbsp oil, 3 tomatoes - pureed in a blender

½ cup curd - beat well till smooth

3 tsp coriander (*dhania*) powder, ¼ tsp dry mango powder (*amchoor*)

½ tsp garam masala, ½ tsp chilli powder (or to taste)

a pinch of turmeric (*haldi*)

2 cloves (*laung*) - crushed, 2 tbsp chopped coriander

1. Pressure cook rajmah, channe ki dal, salt, chopped onion, garlic and ginger together with enough water to give 1 whistle. Keep on low flame for ½ hour. Remove from fire.

2. Heat 4 tbsp oil in a heavy-bottomed kadhai. Add tomatoes pureed in a blender. Cook till tomatoes turn dry.

3. Reduce flame and add dhania powder, amchoor, garam masala, red chilli powder and haldi. Cook till oil separates.

4. Add beaten curd and stir continuously on low flame till the masala turns red again and oil separates.

5. Add crushed laung.

6. Strain and add the rajmah, leaving behind the water. Stir fry on low flame for 5-7 minutes, mashing occasionally.

7. Add the rajmahs to the water in the pressure cooker and pressure cook to give 1 whistle. Keep on low heat for 8-10 minutes. Remove from fire.

8. Garnish with freshly chopped coriander leaves. Serve hot with chappatis or boiled rice.

Water Melon Curry

An unusual curry! Watermelon cubes are simmered in a gravy of watermelon puree, flavoured with spices. Serve with south Indian curd-rice or with plain boiled rice.

Serves 4

4 cups of water melon (*tarbooz*) - cut into 1" pieces along with a little white portion also, and deseeded

4-5 flakes garlic - crushed, ½ tsp cumin seeds (*jeera*), a pinch of asafoetida (*hing*)

2 tbsp oil, 1 tbsp ginger - cut into thin match sticks (juliennes)

½ tsp coriander (*dhania*) powder, ½ - ¾ tsp chilli powder

a pinch of turmeric (*haldi*) powder, ½ tsp salt, or to taste, 2 tsp lemon juice

GARNISH

sliced green chillies & chopped green coriander

1. Puree 1½ cups of water melon cubes (the upper soft pieces) with 4-5 flakes of garlic to get 1 cup of water melon puree. Leave the remaining firm, lower pieces (with the white portion) as it is. Keep aside.

2. Heat 2 tbsp oil in a kadhai or a pan. Add hing and jeera. Let jeera turn golden.

3. Add shredded ginger and stir for ½ minute.

4. Add the remaining water melon pieces or cubes and stir to mix.

5. Sprinkle coriander powder, red chilli powder and haldi. Stir for ½ minute.

6. Add the water melon puree, salt and lemon juice. Simmer for 2-3 minutes till you get a thin curry. Remove from fire.

7. Garnish with green chillies and green coriander. Serve hot with boiled rice.

Dal Makhani

Serves 6

1 cup whole black beans (*urad saboot*), 2 tbsp split gram dal (*channe ki dal*)

2 whole, dry red chillies - soaked in water for 10 minutes, ½" piece ginger, 4 flakes garlic

5 cups of water, 1½ tsp salt, 1 tbsp ghee or oil

4 tomatoes - pureed in a grinder, 2-3 tbsp butter, 1 tbsp kasoori methi

½ tsp garam masala, 2 tsp tomato ketchup, a pinch of orange red colour, optional

½ cup milk, approx., ½ cup fresh cream, ¼ tsp grated nutmeg (*jaiphal*),

1. Grind ginger, garlic and dry red chillies together to a paste. Clean, wash dals. Pressure cook both dals with 5 cups water, 1 tbsp ghee, salt and ginger-garlic-chilli paste. After the first whistle, keep on low flame for 20 minutes. Remove from fire. Keep aside for the pressure to drop.

2. To the boiled dal, add pureed tomatoes, butter, kasoori methi, garam masala and ketchup. Simmer on slow fire for 15 minutes, mashing occasionally. Now add some milk if the dal appears too thick. Cook till it gets the right consistency and colour. Add colour if you wish. Add cream and jaiphal. Serve hot.

Baingan Aur Mirch Ka Saalan

The gravy for this famous dish has sesame seeds, peanuts and coconut and a sharp taste of tamarind – sliced brinjals and green chillies are fried, then simmered in the gravy.

Serves 4

4-5 large, thick green chillies (*achaari hari mirch*)

6 small brinjals - cut into 4 pieces lengthwise and sprinkled with salt

a lemon sized ball of tamarind (*imli*), 5 tbsp oil, ½ tsp mustard seeds (*sarson*)

½ tsp onion seeds (*kalonji*), 3 onions - finely chopped, few curry leaves 2 tbsp fresh cream

GRIND TOGETHER TO A SMOOTH PASTE

2 tbsp sesame seeds (*til*), 2 tbsp peanuts

1 tsp desiccated coconut (coconut powder), optional, 6 flakes garlic, 1½" piece of ginger

2 tsp coriander powder, ¼ tsp turmeric (*haldi*) powder

1 tsp cumin seeds (*jeera*), 1 tsp salt, 1 tsp fresh lemon juice

1. Wash the tamarind & put in a bowl with 1½ cups hot water. Mash and leave it to soak for 10 minutes.

2. Grind the sesame seeds, peanuts, coconut, ginger, garlic, coriander, turmeric, jeera, salt and lemon juice to a paste with a little water. Keep aside.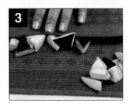

3. Pat dry the brinjals sprinkled with salt on a clean kitchen towel.

4. Heat 5-6 tbsp oil in pan. Reduce heat and fry the green chillies for 1½ minutes. Remove the chillies from the oil and keep aside. In the same oil, add the brinjals. Fry turning sides on medium heat till they change colour and turn brownish. Check with a knife and remove from oil when they turn soft.

5. Heat 2 tbsp oil and add kalonji and sarson. Wait for ½ minute till they crackle, add onions and curry leaves. Fry till onions turn golden brown.

6. Add the freshly ground paste and fry for 1-2 minutes.

7. Add 2 cups water in the pan and stir and then pour strained tamarind juice into the pan. Boil. Simmer for 7-8 minutes on low heat.

8. Add the green chillies and brinjals. Cook for 5 minutes on low heat.

9. Reduce heat. Add cream and remove from fire. Serve with rice or chappati.

INDIAN
DRY
DISHES

Arbi Aur Pyaz ke Lacche

When you don't know what to do with arbi – try this recipe! A fun, light-hearted delight, crisp and tasty.

Serves 4

½ kg calocassia (*arbi*), 2 onions - cut into rings, ½" piece ginger - chopped finely

2 tbsp oil, 2-3 green chillies - cut into long pieces, 2 tomatoes - chopped

¼ tsp turmeric (*haldi*), ½ tsp carom seeds (*ajwain*), ½ tsp cumin seeds (*jeera*)

1 tsp coriander (*dhania*) powder, ½ tsp salt, or to taste

½ tsp red chilli powder, ½ tsp dried mango powder (*amchoor*), ½ cup chopped coriander

1. Pressure cook arbi with 3 cups water with 2 tsp salt to give one whistle. Keep on low flame for 4-5 minutes. Do not over boil. Peel and cut each piece lengthwise into two thin pieces.

2. Heat 2 cups oil in a kadhai for frying. Put 4-5 pieces of flattened arbi at one time in oil. Fry till golden brown. Remove from oil. Keep aside.

3. Heat 2 tbsp oil in a clean kadhai. Reduce flame. Add ajwain and jeera. Cook till jeera turns golden. Add onion rings and cook till soft. Add haldi and mix.

4. Add tomatoes and cook for 2 minutes till soft. Add ginger and stir for a minute.

5. Add chilli powder, amchoor, salt and dhania powder. Stir to mix well. Add 2-3 tbsp water. Boil.

6. Add fried arbi. Mix well. Add chopped coriander and green chillies. Stir fry for 1-2 minutes. Serve.

Note: If the arbi is not boiled in salted water, add a little extra salt.

Subz Paneer Jalfrezi

This jewel-bright presentation of paneer and vegetables is studded with whole spice seeds.

Serves 4

150 gm paneer - cut into thin long pieces, 3 tbsp oil, ½ tsp cumin seeds (*jeera*)

¼ tsp mustard seeds (*sarson*), ¼ tsp onion seeds (*kalonji*)

¼ tsp fenugreek seeds (*methi daana*)

1 firm tomato - cut into 4 pulp removed and cut into thin long pieces

1 large carrot - cut diagonally into thin slices

8-10 french beans - sliced diagonally into 1" pieces

½ green capsicum - deseed and cut into thin fingers

½ yellow or red pepper (capsicum) - deseeded & sliced into thin fingers

15-20 curry leaves

MIX TOGETHER

6 tbsp tomato puree, 1 tbsp tomato ketchup, 2 tsp ginger-garlic paste

½ tsp red chilli powder, 1 tsp coriander (*dhania*) powder

½ tsp dried mango powder (*amchoor*) powder, ¾ tsp salt

1. Heat 3 tbsp oil in a kadhai. Add jeera, sarson, kalonji and methi daana. When jeera turns golden, reduce heat and add curry leaves and stir for a few seconds.

2. Add the tomato puree mixed with dry masalas and stir on medium heat for 2 minutes. Add carrot and beans. Stir for 1 minute. Cover and cook on low heat for about 4-5 minutes, till vegetables are cooked but still remain crunchy.

3. Add the capsicums, paneer and tomato. Stir till well blended. Serve hot.

Til Mil Matar

Sesame seeds are ground into the masala for this dish of green peas. Roasted sesame seeds are tossed on top.

Serves 4

2 cups shelled peas (*matar*) - boiled, 2 tbsp oil, 1 tomato - cut into 8 pieces

2 tbsp dried kasoori methi (fenugreek leaves), 1¼ tsp sesame seeds - dry roasted, to garnish

GRIND TOGETHER WITH A FEW TBSP OF WATER (*MASALA*)

2 onions - roughly chopped, 2 flakes garlic, 2 tsp sesame seeds (*til*)

1 tsp cumin seeds (*jeera*), 1 tsp ground coriander (*dhania powder*)

½ tsp red chilli powder, ¼ tsp turmeric (*haldi*), 1 tsp salt, or to taste

1. To prepare the masala, grind all ingredients with a little water to a fine paste.

2. Heat 2 tbsp oil in a pan or a wok. Reduce heat. Add the masala and fry for about 2 minutes, stirring continuously.

3. Add tomato pieces, boiled peas and kasoori methi. Stir fry for 4-5 minutes on low heat. Serve sprinkled with a few roasted sesame seeds (til).

Bread Dahi Vadas

Soft bread dahi vadas soaked in yogurt and scattered with ginger and green chillies. Impossible to believe they are made from simple slices of white bread! Make them at least half an hour in advance to give them time to soak.

Makes 12

6 slices of fresh bread, 2 cups thick curd (of toned milk) - beat till smooth

¾ tsp roasted cumin powder (*bhuna jeera powder*), ½ tsp red chilli powder

¼ tsp black salt (*kala namak*), 1 tsp salt, a pinch of powdered sugar, or to taste

OTHER INGREDIENTS

1 tbsp finely chopped fresh coriander, 2 green chillies - deseeded and chopped finely

2 tsp ginger juliennes/match stick like pieces, some green (*hari*) chutney and sweet (*meethi*) chutney

2-3 tbsp red fresh pomegranate (*anaar ke daane*), optional

1. Whip curd, add bhuna jeera, red chilli, kala namak, salt and sugar to taste. Keep the raita aside. Cut small rounds from all bread slices.

2. Spread 2-3 tbsp of raita in a shallow rectangular dish. Arrange half of the bread rounds over the raita. Spread 1 tbsp of raita over each piece of bread. Sprinkle a pinch of chopped coriander and green chillies and 1-2 ginger juliennes on it.

3. Spread raita over the remaining bread pieces. Invert them with raita spread down on the arranged pieces on the dish.

4. Pour the left over raita on them to cover completely. With a spoon, pour the chutneys on it, in circles. Garnish with bhuna jeera, red chilli powder, some ginger juliennes and red anar ke daane. Leave in the fridge for at least ½ hour for the bread to soak the curd. Serve with hari chutney & meethi chutney.

KurKuri Ajwaini Bhindi

These are the perfect, crisp ladies' fingers that you have been craving for – flavoured with carom seeds and chaat masala.

Serves 2-3

250 gm lady fingers (*bhindi*), oil for frying, ½ tsp carom seeds (*ajwain*)

¼ tsp turmeric (*haldi*), 2 tsp chaat masala, 3 tbsp gram flour (*besan*)

½ tsp salt, or to taste, juice of ½ lemon (1 tbsp), 1 tsp chilli powder

1. Wash and pat dry bhindi. Cut the head and slit the bhindi into four lengthwise. Place in a shallow bowl or paraat.

2. Heat oil in a kadhai for frying.

3. Sprinkle ajwain, haldi, chaat masala, chilli powder, dry besan and salt on the bhindi.

4. Sprinkle lemon juice and toss well to coat the bhindi.

5. Add half of the bhindi to hot oil and fry in 2 batches till crisp. Drain on absorbent paper. Serve hot with khichree or dal chawal.

Tip: Mix all the ingredients to the bhindi at the time of frying as the salt added releases moisture which can make the bhindi soggy.

To make it really quick, put the oil on fire to get hot. In the meanwhile cut half of the bhindi first and sprinkle half of all the other ingredients and fry the first batch. While the first batch is being fried, cut the left over bhindi.

Karele Lajawab

Bitter gourds are stuffed with mashed potatoes and given a sweet (raisins) and sour (amchoor) touch – guaranteed to increase the number of admirers of this unique vegetable.

Serves 6-8

500 gm (8 - 9) medium bitter gourds (*karelas*)

FILLING

2 large potatoes - boiled & mashed coarsely

½ tsp cumin seeds (*jeera*), 3 tbsp oil

½ tsp mustard seeds (*sarson*), 1 onion - sliced finely

¼ tsp turmeric (*haldi*) powder

½ tsp chilli powder, salt to taste

¾ tsp garam masala

1½ tbsp raisins (*kishmish*) - soaked in water for 15 minutes

1 tsp til - roasted on a griddle (*tawa*) for a minute

1 tomato - chopped, 2 green chillies - deseeded & chopped

2 - 3 tbsp chopped coriander, 1 tsp dried mango powder (*amchoor*)

1. Peel karelas, keeping the stalks intact. Slit. Remove all seeds if they are hard, if not too hard, remove some to make place for the stuffing. Rub salt inside and on the surface of karelas. Keep aside for at least 1 hour.

2. Heat 3 tbsp oil in a kadhai. Reduce flame. Add jeera and sarson. Fry till jeera changes colour.

3. Add onions and fry till transparent. Add salt, red chilli powder, garam masala and haldi powder. Add kishmish and til. Mix.

4. Add tomato, green chillies and coriander. Stir fry for 1- 2 minutes.

5. Add the roughly mashed potatoes and amchoor. Stir fry (Bhuno) for 4-5 minutes on low flame. Remove from fire.

6. Squeeze the karelas, wash a few times. Fill 1-2 tbsp of potato stuffing in each karela. Press to join the sides.

7. Heat 4-5 tbsp oil in a big flat bottomed kadhai. Put in the karelas, one by one gently. Cook uncovered on medium flame for 10-12 minutes, turning them occasionally, to brown them evenly. Cover and cook further for 5 minutes or till soft. Remove from fire & drain out the extra oil. Serve.

Lazeez Aloo Matar

This homely dish has been given a sophisticated make-over with a carefully-phased method of cooking and some lavish ingredients.

Serves 4

4 small sized potatoes - boiled and cut into 2-4 pieces

1 cup boiled or frozen peas

3 tbsp oil, ¾ tsp cumin seeds (*jeera*), 1 large onion - chopped very finely

4-5 cashews - split into halves, 10-15 raisin (*kishmish*) - soaked in water

1 tsp salt, ¼ tsp haldi, ½ tsp garam masala, ½ tsp red chilli powder, ½ tsp dried mango powder (*amchoor*), 2 green chillies - slit lengthwise, 2 tbsp chopped coriander

1. Peel and cut each boiled potato widthwise into 2 equal halves.

2. Heat oil. Add jeera. Wait till it starts changing colour. Add onions. Cook until onions turn light brown. Add kaju. Stir-fry for a minute. Add kishmish.

3. Add salt, haldi, garam masala, red chilli powder and amchoor. Mix.

4. Add potatoes. Stir-fry for 5 minutes on low heat, taking care not to break them. Keep them spaced apart and do not stir too much, so that they turn crisp.

5. Add green chillies and fresh coriander. Cook for 1 minute.

6. Finally, add peas. Mix gently. Cook for 2 minutes stirring occasionally. Remove from fire. Serve hot.

Kadhai Baby Corns

Corns in the usual kadhai masala, flavoured with fenugreek and coriander.

Serves 4

200 gm baby corns (20 pieces approx.)

juice of ½ lemon, 2 capsicums - cut into fingers

1 tomato - deseeded and cut into thin fingers or ½ red capsicum - cut into fingers

1 dry red chilli - deseeded, 1½ tsp coriander seeds (*saboot dhania*), 5 tbsp oil

a pinch of fenugreek seeds (*methi daana*), 2 onions - chopped, 2 tsp ginger-garlic paste

4 tomatoes - blanched and chopped, 1½ tsp salt, or to taste

1 tbsp dried fenugreek leaves (*kasoori methi*), ½ tsp turmeric (*haldi*), ½ tsp garam masala

½ tsp dried mango powder (*amchoor*), 2 tbsp chopped coriander

½" piece ginger - cut into match sticks or shredded on the grater (1 tsp)

1. Boil 4 cups water with 2 tsp salt and lemon juice. Add baby corns and boil for 2 minutes. Drain. Refresh in cold water. Cut into 2 pieces lengthwise, if thick.

2. Warm red chillies and saboot dhania on a tawa, till slightly crisp and dry, for about 30 seconds. Grind red chillies and saboot dhania to a rough powder.

3. Heat 2 tbsp oil in a pan and add the boiled baby corns. Stir for 4-5 minutes till they start turning brown. Keep them spaced out while pan frying and let them not overlap each other. Add the capsicum strips and stir-fry for 2 minutes. Remove from kadhai and keep aside.

4. Heat 3 tbsp oil in a kadhai. Remove from fire. Add a pinch of methi daana, dhania-red chilli powder. Stir for 30 seconds.

5. Return to fire. Add onion. Cook till onions turn light brown. Add garlic-ginger paste. Mix well.

6. Add tomatoes and stir for about 4-5 minutes on low heat till dry.

7. Add salt, kasoori methi, haldi, garam masala and amchoor.

8. Add fresh coriander. Mix well till oil separates. Add ½ cup water. Let it boil. Remove from fire and keep aside till serving time.

9. At the time of serving, add baby corns, tomatoes and capsicum. Cook for 2-3 minutes. Serve hot topped with shredded ginger.

Continental
&
Baked Dishes

Sweet & Sour Cabbage Bake

Make a tomato-based sauce in the Chinese style with vinegar and soya sauce. Pour it over cabbage and bake.

Serves 8

1 medium cabbage (about ½ kg) - cut into 1" squares

4 tomatoes, ½ cup grated carrot (1 big), 3 tbsp oil, 2 tbsp cornflour

1 cup water, 2 tbsp vinegar, 1 tbsp soya sauce, 1 tbsp sugar, 2 tsp salt, or to taste

1. Put tomatoes in boiling water for 3-4 minutes. Remove from water and remove the skin and chop.

2. Heat oil and fry the grated carrot and chopped tomatoes for about 5 minutes. Remove from fire. Let it cool down.

3. Blend tomato-carrots in a mixer. Remove from mixer to a kadhai.

4. To the tomatoes add vinegar, sugar, soya sauce and salt and mix well.

5. Mix cornflour in 1 cup of water and add to the tomato mixture. Cook till the mixture is thick and translucent and a saucy consistency. Keep sauce aside.

6. Cut cabbage into 1" squares. In a greased glass baking dish put the cabbage pieces. Pour over the sweet and sour sauce. Mix gently. Bake in a preheated oven at 180°C for 20-25 minutes or till the cabbage is done.

Potato Layered with Spinach 'n' Corn

This marvellous combination of potato, spinach, corn and cheese will appeal to everyone.

Serves 3- 4

2 cups finely chopped spinach (*palak*)

½ cup corn kernels, 2 onions - finely chopped, 1 tomato - chopped

2 tbsp tomato ketchup, ½ tsp salt, ½ tsp pepper, or to taste

4-5 flakes garlic - crushed, 2 tbsp butter

ALOO & PANEER MASALA

3 potatoes - boiled & grated

150 gm paneer - grated, 2 tbsp finely chopped coriander

2 green chillies - chopped finely

juice of one lemon

½ tsp salt, ½ tsp pepper, 1 tbsp mustard

GARNISHING

4 tbsp grated cheese, 1 firm tomato - sliced

1. Prepare the aloo-paneer masala by mixing all the ingredients well. Keep aside.

2. Heat butter and add crushed garlic. Add finely chopped onion. Fry for 2-3 minutes till light brown. Add tomato. Cook for 1-2 minutes.

3. Add chopped spinach, salt and pepper. Cook for 4-5 minutes.

4. Add corn and tomato ketchup. Mix well. Add a pinch of sugar if required. Remove from fire.

5. Grease a borosil baking dish and spread the aloo-paneer masala at the bottom.

6. Spread spinach and corn over it.

7. Grate cheese over it.

8. Decorate with a row of sliced tomatoes overlapping each other in the centre only. Bake in a hot oven at 200°C/400°F for 15 minutes. Serve hot.

Rice Aubergine Casserole

Rice and fried brinjal slices are layered alternately with a tomato-based red sauce and a cheese sauce – a complete continental meal-in-a-dish!

Serves 4

1 cup rice, 2 bay leaves (*tej patta*), 1 tsp black cumin (*shah jeera*)

1 large round brinjal or aubergine (*bharte waala baingan*) - cut into 1" pieces

1 large capsicum - cut into ½" pieces, oil for frying

RED SAUCE

2 tbsp oil, 1½ onions - chopped, 4 large (400 gm) tomatoes - pureed, 1 tsp oregano

1¼ tsp salt, ¼ tsp pepper, ¼ tsp red chilli powder, ½ tsp sugar

CHEESE SAUCE

1½ tbsp butter, 1½ tbsp plain flour (*maida*)

2 cups milk, 2 cubes (50 gm) cheese - grated, ¾ tsp salt, ¼ tsp pepper

1. Sprinkle ¾ tsp salt on the brinjal. Mix. Keep aside for ½ hour to sweat. Pat dry brinjal on a kitchen towel. Heat oil and deep fry till golden brown. Keep aside.

2. To boil rice, boil 5-6 cups of water with 1 tsp salt, bay leaves & shah jeera. Wash and add rice. Cook till tender. Strain excess water. Run a fork through the hot rice to separate the rice grains. Keep aside.

3. To prepare the red sauce, heat oil. Add chopped onion. Cook till it turns light brown. Add the pureed tomatoes. Add sugar, salt, pepper, red chilli powder and oregano. Cook for about 5 minutes till slightly thick. Remove from heat.

4. For the cheese sauce, heat butter in a clean pan. Add maida and stir on low heat for 1 minute. Add milk and stir continuously till it comes to a boil. Cook for about 2 minutes till it coats the spoon well. Remove from heat. Add cheese, salt and pepper. The sauce should be thin.

5. To assemble, spread half the cooked rice in a medium oven-proof dish. Spread half the aubergines and the chopped capsicum on the rice. Top the brinjals with half the red sauce. Sprinkle half cheese sauce.

6. Again spread rice, then brinjals and then red sauce. Top with cheese sauce and lastly spread capsicums. Cover the dish with an aluminium foil and bake in a preheated oven for 10 minutes at 200°C. Uncover the casserole and bake further for 5 minutes. Serve hot.

Pasta Florentine

Wherever you see the word 'florentine', it means the dish has spinach in some form or the other.

Serves 3-4

3 cups bow-shaped pasta (200 gm) - boiled (5 cups)

4 tbsp butter, 2-3 flakes garlic - crushed, 1 onion - finely chopped

4 cups shredded spinach (½ bunch approx.), 200 ml (1 cup) cream

½ cup grated cheddar cheese (use tin or cubes)

a sprinkle of ground nutmeg (*jaiphal*) powder, ½ tsp salt, ¼ tsp pepper, ½ cup water

1. Melt butter in a pan. Add garlic and onions. Let onions turns golden.

2. Add spinach. Cook for about 7-8 minutes on low heat until dry and soft. Stir occasionally.

3. Keeping the heat low, stir in cream, most of the cheese and nutmeg. Add salt, pepper and water. Boil. Keep aside.

4. At serving time, heat spinach sauce and add pasta. Mix gently until pasta is well coated with sauce. Check salt. Serve sprinkled with some grated cheese.

Chinese

Shredded Potatoes

*Potato fingers are dipped in batter and deep-fried twice to make them wonderfully crisp.
Just before serving they are tossed in a light sauce. Serve as a side dish or a snack.*

Serves 4

2 large potatoes, 3 tbsp cornflour

4-5 green chillies - slit lengthwise and deseeded, 4-5 flakes garlic - crushed, optional

1 tsp soya sauce, 1 tbsp oil, 1 tbsp red chilli sauce, 3 tbsp tomato ketchup

¾ tbsp vinegar, 2 tsp honey, ½ tsp each of salt and white pepper

3 spring onions - white part finely chopped & greens cut diagonally into 2" pieces

BATTER

¼ cup flour (*maida*), ¼ cup cornflour, ½ tsp salt

¼ tsp pepper, ½ tsp soya sauce, a pinch or drop of orange red colour

1. Wash and peel the potatoes. Cut into ¼" thick slices. Cut each slice into ¼" wide fingers. Soak them in 4-5 cups cold water with 2 tsp salt and juice of 1 lemon, for 15 minutes. Strain and wipe dry on a clean kitchen towel. Sprinkle ¼ tsp pepper and 3-4 tbsp cornflour on them to absorb excess water.

2. For batter- mix flour, cornflour, salt, pepper, soya sauce and colour. Add just enough water, about 5-6 tbsp, to make a batter of a thick pouring consistency, so that it coats the potatoes.

3. Dip fingers of potatoes in the batter and deep fry to a golden orange colour. Check that they get properly cooked on frying. Keep aside, spread out on a plate till the time of serving.

4. Heat 1 tbsp oil in a pan. Add white of spring onion. Stir till light brown. Remove from fire. Add the green chillies and garlic. Stir till garlic changes colour.

5. Add soya sauce, chilli sauce, tomato ketchup and vinegar.

6. Return to fire. Stir for 30 seconds to cook the sauces. Add honey.

7. Add salt and pepper. Remove from fire. Keep aside.

8. At serving time, heat oil for refrying the potatoes. Add the fried potatoes in hot oil and refry for a minute. Remove from oil and put in the pan of sauces. Add spring onion greens. Mix very well for a minute on high heat. Check salt. Serve.

Chilli Garlic Noodles

These quick and easy stir-fried noodles will tickle your taste buds with their strong garlic and chilli flavour – serve with any sauce-based main dish.

Serves 3-4

200 gm dried noodles, 3 tbsp oil, 1 tbsp crushed garlic

3 dry, whole red chillies - broken into bits

½ tsp red chilli flakes, ½ tsp salt or to taste, 1 tsp soya sauce

1. To boil noodles, in a large pan, boil 10-12 cups water with 2 tsp salt and 1 tbsp oil. Add noodles to boiling water.

2. Cook uncovered, on high flame for about 2-3 minutes only. Stir once in between.

3. Remove from fire before they get overcooked. Drain. Wash with cold water several times.

4. Strain. Leave them in the strainer for 15-20 minutes, turning them upside down, once after about 10 minutes to ensure complete drying. Apply 1 tsp oil on the noodles and spread in a tray till further use.

5. Cut the dry red chillies into small bits or pieces.

6. Heat 3 tbsp oil. Add garlic. Stir. Remove from fire, add broken red chillies and red chilli flakes.

7. Return to fire and mix in the boiled noodles. Add salt and a little soya sauce. Mix well with the help of 2 forks. Fry for 2-3 minutes, till the noodles turn a pale brown. Serve hot.

Sticky Rice with Peas

Sticky rice, honey and soya sauce show a Chinese origin – cumin, coriander and aniseed (saunf) tell you that it is Made in India!

Serves 6

1½ cups uncooked sticky rice (new short grained rice may be used), 2 tbsp oil

1 onion - sliced, 2 flakes garlic - crushed

2 spring onions - chop white and green part separately

2 green chillies - chopped, ½ cup peas (*matar*), ½ tsp cumin powder (*jeera powder*)

½ tsp ground coriander (*dhania*) powder, 1 tsp saunf - crushed, 1 tsp salt, ½ tsp pepper

HONEY STOCK

3 cups veg stock or 3 cups of water mixed with 1 vegetable seasoning cube

3 tbsp honey, 3 tbsp soya sauce

1. Wash and soak rice. Keep aside.

2. Mix all the ingredients for the honey stock in a bowl. Keep aside.

3. Heat oil in a large deep pan, add sliced onion & garlic and stir-fry for 4-5 minutes or until onion is soft.

4. Add white part of spring onion, green chillies and peas.

5. Add jeera powder, dhania powder, crushed saunf, salt and pepper. Stir-fry for 1 minute.

6. Drain rice and add to the pan. Stir for 3-4 minutes on low heat.

7. Add honey-stock mixture and green of spring onion. Stir and bring to a boil.

8. Reduce heat and cook covered for 10 minutes on low heat or until rice is done and the water gets absorbed. Serve hot.

Veggies in Hot Garlic Sauce

Serves 3-4

100 gm tofu or paneer - cut into ¼" thick triangular pieces - sprinkled with ¼ tsp salt &
white pepper and 1 tbsp cornflour, 4-5 florets of broccoli or cauliflower, 4 tbsp oil

4-6 babycorns - cut into 2 pieces lengthwise

1 carrot - sliced very diagonally and then cut into 2 pieces

6-8 leaves of bokchoy or spinach

1 tbsp of dried black mushrooms or 3-4 fresh mushrooms - cut into 2 pieces

1 capsicum - cut into 1" pieces

GARLIC SAUCE

20 flakes garlic and 2 dry, red chillies (soaked) - crushed to a rough paste

3 tbsp oil, ½ onion - cut into 4 pieces and separated, 4 tbsp tomato ketchup

2 tsp red chilli sauce, 2 tsp soya sauce, ½ tsp pepper, 1 tsp salt, a pinch sugar

2 tsp vinegar, 1½ cups water

3 tbsp cornflour mixed with ½ cup water

1. If using dried black mushrooms, put them in a pan. Cover with water. Boil. Simmer for 2 minutes. Remove from fire. Keep aside for 10 minutes. Wash several times to remove dirt. Break off any hard stem portion and discard. Cut into smaller pieces. If using bokchoy or spinach, trim the stem, remove any discoloured leaves. Tear into 2" pieces.

2. Boil 4-5 cups water with 1 tsp salt. Remove from fire. Add broccoli or cauliflower, baby corns, carrots and bokchoy or spinach. Leave veggies in hot water for 1-2 minutes and strain. Refresh in cold water and keep aside till serving time.

3. Heat 4 tbsp oil in a pan. Shallow fry the tofu till golden. Remove tofu from pan.

4. Heat 3 tbsp oil. Remove from fire. Add garlic and red chilli paste. Stir till garlic starts to change its colour. Add onion cubes, stir for a minute.

5. Add tomato ketchup, red chilli sauce, soya sauce, pepper and salt. Cook for 1 minute on low heat. Add sugar and vinegar.

6. Add soaked mushrooms, blanched vegetables and capsicum. Stir.

7. Add water, give one boil. Add cornflour paste, stirring all the time. Cook for 2 minutes on low heat. Remove from heat. Keep sauce aside. At serving time, add fried tofu to sauce & boil for 2 minutes. Serve with rice.

Rice
& Bread

Instant Paneer Kulche

Makes 8

½ cup semolina (*suji*), ¼ cup water (for soaking semolina), 1 tsp sugar

2 cups (200 gm) flour (*maida*), 1½ tsp baking powder, 1 tsp salt, ½ cup water

FILLING (MIX TOGETHER)

1 cup grated or mashed paneer (100 gm), 2 tbsp chopped coriander

2 tsp chopped green chillies, ½ tsp red chilli powder, ¼ tsp salt, ¼ tsp black pepper

1. Mix suji and sugar. Add ¼ cup water and mix well. Keep aside for 15 minutes.

2. Sieve maida, salt and baking powder. Add sugar and suji mix and mix well. Add enough water to lightly gather the mixture into a soft dough. Do not knead.

3. Apple some oil on the dough and cover with a moist cloth. Rest the dough for at least 20 minutes or more. Divide dough into 8 balls and cover them.

4. Cover the tray of an electric tandoor with aluminium foil. Grease foil. Heat the tandoor. Take one ball, flatten with your hand. Keep the filling in the center and

close it up as you do for stuffed paranthas. Roll it like a chappati using maida. Dust off the extra maida.

5. Place kulche on the lined tray. Put the tray with kulcha back in the hot tandoor. Cook till light golden specks appear on the kulche. Serve hot greased with butter.

Ajwaini Daal Parantha

Flavour any left-over dal with carom seeds (ajwain) then add just enough wheat flour (atta) to bind into a dough – make quick paranthas and use up left-overs!

Serves 2-3

1 cup leftover cooked dal

1¼-1½ cups wheat flour (*atta*), or as required, ½ tsp carom seeds (*ajwain*)

½ tsp garam masala, ½ tsp salt, or to taste, 1 green chilli - chopped finely

2 tbsp green coriander - chopped

1. Mix all the ingredients in a shallow bowl (paraat). Knead to a soft dough without using any water, so add just enough atta to get a proper dough.

2. Roll out a thick chappati and smear little ghee. Fold again into a ball. Roll out to a round parantha.

3. Heat a tawa and cook parantha on both sides. Add a little ghee on one side and overturn. Press the top and sides of the parantha with a large spoon or karchhi to get a crisp parantha. Serve with curd.

Spicy Tomato Rice

Cooked rice is transformed into a flavourful medley to serve on any occasion.

Serves 4

3 cups boiled rice

3-4 tbsp chopped coriander leaves, 2 tbsp oil, 1 tsp oregano or ¾ tsp carom seeds (*ajwain*)

2 big onions - finely chopped, 6 tbsp tomato puree, 1 tbsp tomato ketchup

1½ tsp salt or to taste, 1 tsp red chilli powder

¾ tsp freshly ground peppercorns (*saboot kaali mirch*)

---

1. Heat oil in a big kadhai or a wok. Reduce flame. Add oregano or ajwain.

2. After a few seconds, add onions and stir fry till light brown.

3. Add tomato puree. Cook for 1 minute.

4. Reduce flame. Add tomato ketchup, red chilli powder, salt and pepper.

5. Add the rice. Stir fry gently for 2 minutes.

6. Add chopped coriander. Mix well. Check salt and pepper. Serve hot.

Lemon Rice

Cooked rice is made deliciously lemony in a jiffy – fresh curry leaves and mustard seeds add to the turmeric-coloured lively appearance.

Serves 4

3 cups boiled rice - spread on a tray for grains to separate, juice of 2 lemons

¼ tsp turmeric (*haldi*) powder, 1 tsp sugar, 1½ tsp salt or to taste

TEMPERING (*CHOWNK*)

2 tbsp oil, 1 tsp mustard seeds (*sarson*), 1 tbsp split gram dal (*channe ki dal*)

3 dry, red chillies - broken into pieces, few curry leaves

1. Mix lemon juice, haldi, salt and sugar together in a small bowl.

2. Heat oil in kadhai. Reduce flame. Add sarson, dal & red chillies. Cook on very low flame till dal just starts changing colour. Do not let the dal turn brown.

3. Add curry leaves. Add the lemon juice mixture. Add ¼ cup water. Cover and simmer on low flame till dal turns soft and the water dries.

4. Add rice and stir gently till well mixed for 2-3 minutes. Serve hot.

Garlic Bread Loaf

Garlic butter mixed with fresh herbs is spread generously to make this bread a hot favourite with all ages.

Serves 8

1 french loaf

6 tbsp butter softened, 1 tbsp lemon juice, 1 tsp crushed garlic

2 tbsp grated cheddar cheese, ½ tsp mixed herb or oregano

1 tbsp fresh parsley or coriander

1. Slit loaf into ½" thick slices, leaving the loaf attached at the bottom.

2. To prepare the spread, beat butter till fluffy. Mix all the other ingredients.

3. Spread the herbed butter inside each slit. If some butter is left, spread on top. Wrap loaf in an aluminium foil, sealing the edges well.

4. Preheat oven at 200°C for 20 minutes and bake the foil-covered loaf.

5. At serving time, open foil from top and bake for another 5 minutes.

Sweet
Delights

Rasgulla Surprise

Boil milk till it reduces, thicken with coconut and cornflour and flavour with saffron – pour over readymade rasgullas and surprise your guests!

Serves 4

4 ready-made rasgullas - cut each into 2 pieces

¼ tsp saffron (*kesar*) dissolved in 3 tbsp warm milk for 10 minutes, 2½ cups milk

1 tbsp sugar, 1 packet coconut powder (maggie) or 2 tbsp desiccated coconut

2 tbsp cornflour mixed with ½ cup milk, a few almonds/pistas - chopped, to garnish

1. Boil milk in a heavy-bottomed kadhai. Cook on low medium flame for 15-20 minutes, stirring frequently. Keep scraping the sides of the kadhai too.

2. Add coconut powder, dissolved kesar and sugar. Mix.

3. Add cornflour paste. Mix well stirring for a few seconds. Remove from fire. Cool.

4. Add halved rasgullas, mix. Keep aside in the fridge till serving time. Garnish with chopped almonds and pistas. Serve cold.

Badaam Stuffed Lychees

A very decorative & a delicious dessert with an Indian flavour. Assure your guests that the seed of the fruit has been removed and replaced with a blanched almond to enjoy the fruit comfortably.

Serves 8-10

20-25 large lychees, 20-25 almonds - blanched (soaked in hot water & skin removed) 2-3 sheets of silver sheets (*warq*)

½ tin of milkmaid (condensed milk) (¾ cup), 250 gm paneer - grated

¼ tsp saffron (*kesar*) - soaked in 1 tbsp rose water

300 gm cream - chilled nicely and whipped till it turns thick

1. Peel and carefully deseed the lychees, keeping the lychees whole.

2. Insert one almond in each lychee in place of the seed.

3. Open up a varak carefully. Place 3-4 lychees on the sheet leaving some space in-between the lychees. Carefully lift the paper beneath the varak to coat the lychees with varak. Do not touch the varak directly. Keep some plain and some covered with silver sheet. Refrigerate lychees.

4. Whip the chilled cream (chill the cream before whipping) till slightly thick.

5. Beat ½ tin condensed milk and saffron along with the rose water in a pan till smooth. Add the grated paneer and mix well.

6. Add cream to the condensed milk mixture to get a kheer like consistency of the mixture (thick pouring consistency). If you like it less sweet, add some more grated paneer. Transfer to a shallow serving dish. Top mixture with lychees.

Fruity Chocolate Squares

These chilled morsels have crushed biscuits, raisins and thick luscious chocolate; they can be decorated with any seasonal fruit – gourmet class but so easy to make!

Serves 10

200 gm marie biscuits (crushed into very tiny pieces)

¼ cup black raisins (*kishmish*)

200 gm cooking chocolate - cut into small pieces

100 gm cream, ½ tsp vanilla essence

3-4 strawberries or 1 kiwi

1. Crush biscuits and mix essence with it. Add raisins.

2. Heat cream on very low heat in a heavy-bottomed pan. Add chocolate pieces to it. Mix it well till chocolate melts. Remove from fire and stir well to make a smooth sauce.

3. Mix a little more than half of the sauce with the crushed biscuits, just enough to bind the mixture nicely.

4. Line a loaf tin with aluminium foil and put the mixture into it. Press and level it with your hands. Keep in the freezer for 10 minutes till set.

5. Demould the set biscuits on a wire rack. Place a plate underneath the rack. Heat the remaining sauce, if need be with a tbsp of water and pour on the set biscuit mixture. Level the sauce on the sides with palatte knife and keep it back in the fridge for 10-15 minutes to set.

6. Cut into 2" square pieces and decorate it with any sliced of fresh fruit of your choice & serve chilled.

Ice Cream Trifle

Use lots of imagination and some readymade ingredients to assemble a trifle made of cake, ice cream and fresh fruit.

Serves 8

3-4 black forest pastries or any other pastries

1 tin mixed tinned fruit or 2 cups chopped fresh fruits

1 family pack (500 ml) vanilla ice cream, 1-2 tbsp chocolate sauce to top

a few almonds - cut into thin long pieces

1. Cut the pastries into thin slices. Place them in a shallow serving dish covering the bottom of the dish. Take a knife and spread the cream evenly on the pastries.

2. Soak the pastries with 4-5 tbsp of the mixed fruit syrup (should feel slightly moist). If using fresh fruit, soak the pastries with cold milk.

3. Spread the drained, canned fruit or chopped fresh fruit on the pastries.

4. At serving time, top the fruit with scoops of ice cream.

5. Pour a few swirls of chocolate sauce on the ice cream. Decorate with almonds.

Glossary of Names/Terms

HINDI OR ENGLISH NAMES as used in India	USED IN USA/UK/OTHER COUNTRIES
Amchoor	Dried mango powder
Baingan	Eggplant, aubergine
Chhoti Elaichi	Green cardamom
Chilli powder	Red chilli powder, Cayenne pepper
Cornflour	Cornstarch
Dalchini	Cinnamon
Hara Dhania	Cilantro/fresh or green coriander
Hari Mirch	Green hot peppers, green chillies
Imli	Tamarind
Kalonji	Onions seeds
Methi dana	Fenugreek seeds
Sarson	Mustard seeds
Saunf	Fennel
Seviyaan	Vermicelli
Shah jeera	Black cumin
Til	Sesame seeds

INTERNATIONAL CONVERSION GUIDE

These are not exact equivalents; they've been rounded-off to make measuring easier.

WEIGHTS & MEASURES

METRIC	IMPERIAL
15 g	½ oz
30 g	1 oz
60 g	2 oz
90 g	3 oz
125 g	4 oz (¼ lb)
155 g	5 oz
185 g	6 oz
220 g	7 oz
250 g	8 oz (½ lb)
280 g	9 oz
315 g	10 oz
345 g	11 oz
375 g	12 oz (¾ lb)
410 g	13 oz
440 g	14 oz
470 g	15 oz
500 g	16 oz (1 lb)
750 g	24 oz (1½ lb)
1 kg	30 oz (2 lb)

LIQUID MEASURES

METRIC	IMPERIAL
30 ml	1 fluid oz
60 ml	2 fluid oz
100 ml	3 fluid oz
125 ml	4 fluid oz
150 ml	5 fluid oz (¼ pint/1 gill)
190 ml	6 fluid oz
250 ml	8 fluid oz
300 ml	10 fluid oz (½ pint)
500 ml	16 fluid oz
600 ml	20 fluid oz (1 pint)
1000 ml	1¾ pints

CUPS & SPOON MEASURES

METRIC	IMPERIAL
1 ml	¼ tsp
2 ml	½ tsp
5 ml	1 tsp
15 ml	1 tbsp
60 ml	¼ cup
125 ml	½ cup
250 ml	1 cup

HELPFUL MEASURES

METRIC	IMPERIAL
3 mm	1/8 in
6 mm	¼ in
1 cm	½ in
2 cm	¾ in
2.5 cm	1 in
5 cm	2 in
6 cm	2½ in
8 cm	3 in
10 cm	4 in
13 cm	5 in
15 cm	6 in
18 cm	7 in
20 cm	8 in
23 cm	9 in
25 cm	10 in
28 cm	11 in
30 cm	12 in (1ft)

Nita Mehta's NEW RELEASES

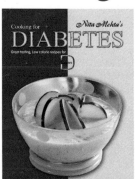

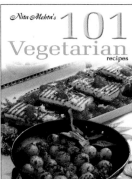

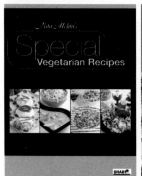